D1203045

Gallery Books
Editor Peter Fallon

DULSE

Frank McGuinness

DULSE

Frank Mc-
Guinness

Gallery Books

Dulse
is first published
simultaneously in paperback
and in a clothbound edition
on 14 December 2007.

The Gallery Press
Loughcrew
Oldcastle
County Meath
Ireland

www.gallerypress.com

*All rights reserved. For permission
to reprint or broadcast these poems,
write to The Gallery Press.*

© Frank McGuinness 2007

ISBN 978 1 85235 437 4 *paperback*
    978 1 85235 438 1 *clothbound*

A CIP catalogue record for this book
is available from the British Library.

Contents

in memory of Joan O'Hara

Korea

I am the Korean archery champ.
I spend my life sending arrows northwards.

To each I attach a token of love:
unicorn feathers, alcohol-free beer,

invitations to a party of rice cakes,
birthday suit, raw fish, ground-up light bulbs.

This last is a delicacy reserved
to improve eyesight: the bow from the quiver

that travels straight from the heart to the head,
heart of Korea, head of the arrow.

Blackrock Park

The swans have deserted.
They leave the pond for Tír-na-nÓg.
But age fetters them.
They eat their young.
Their feathers are red
ice cream, their wings hems.

When their young are eaten,
then they marry well.
They disperse, pure heathens
who feed on gems.
Born under the sign of the ram,
what tales have they to tell,
breathing through the lace of stays,
breathing through the skin of shark?

Lose your way through this maze
you wake and walk in Blackrock Park.

Beget that book in the Bible
where swans kiss and tell.

Emmaus

for Paul Bates

I believe in the disappearing act.
The breathing of stones — the stealth that is bread —
the resurrection of wine: Emmaus.

I believe in supping with Somalis —
Vikings playing ivory chess — a shy
electric guitar singing Beatles songs.

I believe second love is possible —
love ordering itself in restaurants,
love red as Mexico, as Emmaus.

I believe a diver connects ocean
to firmament in Winchester Cathedral —
the saving grace, the abiding rainbow.

I believe in not weeping when tears drown
the North Sea, the Baltic; every sea
separates self and soul from my love.

I believe the act of disappearing
may involve the breathing of stone, of bread.
My heart is that broken bread, broken stone.

Samurai

The railway line
a feast of ghosts,
Pound Lane Bridge their shell.

I carry milk
in a silver can
and make my bets.

The world will be spared,
Hiroshima won't happen,
if I reach home.

I meet Buncrana samurai —
who put that weapon
into their hard mitts?

Why are they flaying
a hunting gun
they raise and point

to take the eye out
of an electric light,
spilling yellow seed?

Shiny with milk,
my white hands smell
as Eros bleeds.

I cross the bridge.

The Sugar Daddy

Years before she was invented
my rich widow chewed toffee
cracking the brown slabs
into a strange confection —
her husband's broken promise
never to remarry.

How sour it would all turn,
sour as marsh water
hiding her disappeared,
our phantom son
by this errant master —
child that never was.

Wading through his grave
up to her strong oxsters
the mare of Flanders wept
tears of sticky substance
which her sugar daddy
lavished on his hounds.

The Tale of the Maid who Turned

My bones I hang on nails,
my flesh I dress for Sunday.
The house is polished red,
the garden plaits its rainy hair
with dirty streels of honey
and bees wax the flowers.

I serve a clergyman, fierce
altogether, he takes no nonsense,
looks at me like a creature
not in touch with earth's orbit.

My fingers smell of butcher meat
seven times knived, seven times
cooked in a giant oven;
fished from nature mussels
mixed themselves with oyster shells,
crabtoed fresh herring.

With teeth still sharp and long legs
I run rings around the men
wanting bread in freezing rooms
next door to my body.

It stood in front of windows
and Master took a shine
to my lovely reflection.
A bullet put paid to that,
the gun apeing its betters.

I saw glass bend the knee
at the feet of ladies
spilling like strong whiskey

wasted on laps
that stained bright as red
children being born.

Shelling peas and stripping beans
of their sour protective skins
I thought to my silent self
it's time to turn religion.
I know how bread is buttered.

We die in dangerous times.
More fool I if I let myself
be thrown out of heaven
for the sake of eggs and bacon
but I still lick my plate.

I fetch quick as I can carry
down backstairs into chambers
where fires in warm corners
burn the logs of Ireland
bereft of print or thumb mark.

I work while midges eat me,
the vestments of the devil
buzzing in priestly Latin
reading my confession out,
a girl's tragic turning.

Were I to perish in service
browning toast and baking shapes
making up beds and shakedowns —
a shame we have to sleep
and graze and drink and drouth —

I would slip through the rafters,
the banisters and doorstep,
dressed in the robe a goddess
carved with stony tresses
guards this heathen valley.

In Memory of John McGahern

He wipes the clay of Leitrim from his lips
but it returns to lodge in the white star
of the train that takes him westward, eastward,
all which ways that flood the lakes of Leitrim.

He bathes in the Ganges of their blessing
and sacrilegious fields; heathen cattle
turn him heretic and gentle. John,
they are your due, the fields, the lips, the clay.

Mary Holland Met with Death

He asked her for three wishes.
She refused the greedy gut.
Mary Holland said to Death:

You will not strike me dumb.
I don't follow your fashion.
The sway of you, the look, the cut.
I warn you, I'll give you the lash.

Death took a gun into the forest
to kill a swan both white and black —
the bird had paid no heed to weapons
that turned the forest sky to ash.
Death asked our woman with no mask:

You devoured life — its crust, its crumb —
you pride yourself, you answer back,
so is first first and last last
when you wake from the sleep of reason?

After Catullus

for Ronan Sheehan

1 VIBENNIUS AND SON

Watch that old boy, Vibennius,
he'd steal the skin from your ass.
His son prefers gander to goose —
we've all parked up his cul-de-sac.
The whole world knows the daddy's doings,
no shame on him, no hiding place.
But I begin to pity the young buck,
his arse hairy as a jungle.
Past it now, he'd piss for a penny —
Sorry, pal, no takers anymore.

2 SWEET IPSTILLA

Come on, sweet mouth,
you who could charm
the trees from the birds.
Your breath is a butterfly —
you know what I want.
What's keeping you? Ring me.
Let's make love in the afternoon.
I need to — I need it now.
If you want to fuck we'll fuck.
My hand's hard with the motion
stoning drawers and trousers.

The Herring Gutters

At the pier in red scarves
the women gut herring.
They smell of work,
they earn their pay.
They share a chorus
of 'Slievenamon'.

Alone, all alone,
the garrison
of soldier boys
in British uniforms —
Buncrana is safe
in times of war.

The green of a girl's
ghost, her dress bleeds
green, shot by God knows,
skipping a rope,
seen by herring gutters,
haunts this town.

Jet black hair, one hides
against her breast
the secret order —
flesh for flesh, bone for bone —
and delivers safely
a son to a gun.

Poisonous entrails
slit and discarded
by their fierce knives
leave fish safe
for human consumption.
Buncrana is fed.

Ur

Fresh milk from the plains of Islamic Armagh
quenched the thirst of circumcised alcoholics
who once had the gumption to rise and poke sticks
at brutes and beasts dolled to the nines, ra-ra
skirts up, body stockings down, shaved of all hair
raising Cain cross the border in the land of Nod,
dirtying the temples of Chaldean gods
carousing till cocks crowed the fate of Ur.

Five-fingered Strand

I met a man
who met his fate
on Five-fingered Strand.

He led his wife
a merry dance;
he was taking a hand.

I do, my love,
bequeath to you
all my worldly goods:

my body's frame,
a daisy chain,
my coffin, my pram.

She whispered back,
I do receive
all that you leave to me

but spare me, please,
the dying breath,
the stench of wild thyme.

He smiled, he smelt
just where he stood
extinct as eyebright.

Vodka and Coke

After an early night
you, the lover of lost years,
I touch
with some degree of tenderness —
I want to ask,
Am I that bad?

Knowing I hate liars,
you would swear
that peace is a wedding gift,
something to bless
and not to break.
Quiet is better than mad.

Your fist would not rise.
You would fall asleep.
In the vodka and coke
of dreams I hear you weep.

Sheet

Two sheets engaged in violent sex.
They tumbled — tore the joint apart.
They left the shirts a savage mess.
They separated chaff from chaff
into rainbowed smithereens,
angelic warlike white beneath us.

The Moon-calf

The moon wondered, Why don't I marry?
I said it was because I had no babies.
That was how we practised circumcision.
Bed was a place of low peaks and red valleys.
I stopped exploring its wide farthest reaches —
put it down to the fear of conceiving.
That's why I'd never dream of writing novels,
why I would never travel alone.
My paid companion altered her real name.
She even changed sex, indulged in sorrow,
and took to pills like doctors to whiskey,
waddling through fat seasons, bacon and cabbage,
till her mouth took a tumbling from the dish
of babes and innocents and pink paper.

The pink of the paper demanded reasons.
It believed in the pure power of reason.
Expressing itself as it excelled itself,
turning black where it should choose to turn black.
Believing in music, in the moon-calf,
it did the rounds, sucking on men's nipples,
dreaming of milk in white alabaster veins,
dining on lilacs, a poison of heather.
It thrived in climes of Antarctic beauty,
aware it was born where it should have died.
The drugs kept it going, morphine its meat.
And the moon-calf did survive, the moon-calf
bought its freedom, found a wife, married well
to men who said, Yes. There were no babies.

Galleon

for Dorothy Cross

Last night I dreamt my father drowned, leaping
into the Atlantic of his ghost grave
from a galleon that sailed becalmed waters
around the islands of forgetfulness
where we both grew up, master and potboy,
the devilish reflection of each other.
I prayed to rain for my father's soul
so it may thrive in extreme conditions
and prosper as it deserved to prosper
there where galleons took root and settled
bringing a cargo of amusing natives
across the Swilly fjord to Rathmullan.
Performing rituals of abasement
that would turn the head and disgrace the tongue,
those same godfearing, godforsaken people
held on to the shirtsleeves of my father
begging him not to desert the ship —
but, stubborn captain, he chose to abandon.
To this day the spot he drowned in my dream
is known as the deep of deepest sorrow.

The Black Farm

In the salt cold
of delighted water
nuns in grey costume
are swimming near
the black farm.
As for Satan, no fear
has ever touched their souls
to sing the blues
if they marry,
making Atlantic stew
from the salt cold
of delightful water.

At the black farm
where Satan's dreaming
the servant girls
bought at hiring fairs
ply valium
and round squares
to timid pilgrims
dreaming of home.
They'd shed the shell,
they dream of bones
at the black farm
where Satan's dreaming.

In the black farm
of delighted water,
in the salt cold
where Satan's dreaming,
he will see the sun
on fire and, beaming,
he'll find his love
who is warm and true,
and they will marry

making Atlantic stew
in the black farm
of delightful water.

Bread

E m'è pane quel boccio di velluto.

— Montale

I glance back
at boulders,
at furrows,
my Donegal bread.

It is like velvet
or silk you feed
to mad birds
and crazy swallows.

They are mandolins
in black flight.
Bread from this world
that sustains me.

I follow.

Brendan O'Dowda

Long, long ago Brendan O'Dowda's voice
is like a safe house to a flash rebel son
running for his life through rich plantation
counties down Mexico way where cowboys
in white vests pitchcap their tarred, their feathered prey.

The Doctor's Daughter in Antwerp

for Julie and Tom Kilroy

My father was mad enough to work miracles.
He modelled himself on dear Jeanne d'Arc.
His patients were practical, hearing his voices.
They believed in a god that healed pain.
The same god was obsessed with suffering.
My father thought suffering a purple rose.
Invited to weddings, my father blessed peasants
nearly ready to deliver children. They'd knock
at back doors my mother answered, calmly, kind.

When I was young poverty in Antwerp,
like shite on the doorstep, was everywhere.
Morning stung me. I'd hear hoofs of workers' sabots
scratch against cobblestone. They were tomcats
returned after hunting, with blood sleeping
in their arms, their fine four legs, their eyed faces.
I'd turn over, I'd go into iced sleep.
Sunday velvet touched the tip of their clogs.
They were washed and scrubbed. The smell of the sink
turned this town into something clean. Holy well.

Pilgrims came to our house, women abandoned —
they'd walk on bare knees from Antwerp to Mechlin,
thanksgiving for a child my father saved.
Was my father god? He drank fat red wine
smelling of salt and a hand fierce gypsies fed
to pay him for medicine that did no good
but brought the rough consolation of science
to hard lumps in the breast which should have been seen
before my faith started bleeding. Wounds of Christ
filled my father with mercy. He tried his best.

Was his best enough?
Looked at through its reflection, the station
in Antwerp is railway green, is red sorrow
on the way to the waiting room in Mechlin.
We've made many times the journey to Brussels.
We've cursed many times the train's late arrival,
hungry for scallops, spinach and white rice,
skeletal poussin, sweet Sancerre — laughing water.
Imagine the journey home. We're music, safe
in Antwerp, our railway station stained glass,
my sorrowful father working miracles.

I am his daughter, the doctor's daughter.
I no longer believe in Belgium nor in God.
But I pray that Jeanne d'Arc hear my voices
waiting in Mechlin, my vomiting nights.
I pray — do not stop at the station in Mechlin,
let my dreams be tales from Copenhagen.
A king saw his heart like a golden star.
From his body he plucked eternal fire.
And a cat in the shape of a flower blossomed
on the grave where he slept beside my father.

We have known hard times and nearly starved.
We've been drenched by rain near cathedrals.
Iconoclasts broke beautiful stained glass.
I gather shards and fashion them into my father.
I say to him, You are forgiven, you who died,
who did your best, who did not work miracles.
I remember who I am when I think of you.
Am I the doctor's daughter from Antwerp?
Some nights a cat in the shape of a flower
comes from Siam, whispering of Mechlin.

The Shrine of the Three Wise Men, Köln

BALTHAZAR

As a child on that island
drenched to the skin
by gods of fear
I lashed out
at shins and knees
of high priests
and their lackeys
worshipping death
in the guise of
half-mad sea creatures.
Come the night
they would lap themselves
ashore and sing
oceanic lullabies
to the moon.
They had escaped
before bedtime,
before dreams
in the shape of a star.
My two feet
abolished their power,
racing somewhere foreign
to Bethlehem.
I was content
to be there,
bones at the shrine.

CASPAR

To my watchful eye
the Rhine looked calm,
surveyed from the distance
where three of us stand.
It is treacherous
water, perhaps
it will stab us all
if we remain.
Maybe it will tell us
the secrets sought
by travellers more ancient
than we kings
of orient and peninsula,
we who plough
the furrows of lonely rock
and lazy bones,
long inclined to bend
knee and dance,
illuminated,
by Rhine light.

MELCHIOR

I know a country
where they bury the dead
alive in their rubble
left behind by wind
and fire and glass
that restored sweet breath
to unfortunate sons
wandering earth.
The city of Köln
bears witness
to smoke and shadows,
signs of the times,
gold, myrrh, frankincense,
the shepherds nicked
together with angels singing.
I know a city
where we praise the dead,
much like my own
in the ancient clay.

The High Balcony

If I had money I'd take you
to the high balcony, you so worldly,
not the kind to take an overdose,
spilling tablets all over the carpet.
I would be content to bottle up
the monthly feelings that I script
from top to bottom, a Minoan
secret, deciphering the bullshit
I should take neither art nor part —
art nor part I should push aside,
concentrate instead on bombing raids,
navigating along the chartered plans.
My instruments burst with idealism,
dambusting, creating the high balcony.

A girl whose secret blood I shared,
she's died in Spain's Valencia;
the city's harbour froze to bone,
clicked its fingers, called her home.
The Atlantic wanted to let rip
but she confined its bullish passions.
She walked, this girl, my fearless cousin,
unscathed through nature's labyrinth,
her laughter protecting from harm
her skin-white flesh, her reddening hair.
She would know the high balcony,
the pleasant vision of the Alps,
a sojourn, say, near Lake Geneva —
she went there for her heart and health.

If I'd my way I would construct
the artifice of high balconies.
The builders would be secret drinkers
retiring to sleep, to starve for the night
on beds of ice and Viking lace.

They'd melt each and every morning
and pass away like bloodsick girls
who lose the will to live, to fight.
I could demonstrate the proof
that love is a lost inflection,
a varied, knowing conjugation,
a shifting vowel, a rich grammar.
That's why we do what we most desire —
we fly down from the high balcony.

Fly down from the air to darkest earth.
The whole globe is heavenly grid —
a melt of star and shift and Asia
that conforms to the name of towns
that lost their meaning years ago.
The words for boy, the word for girl
could no longer be translated
into modern, Minoan speech.
I can read Valentian script,
lamenting my lost cousin's soul.
Were I engaged in excavating
the legends of her suffering
I would set up camp and comfort
in the confines of high balconies.

A solution presented itself:
I spoke in lost dialects,
archaic, defective, explaining
to the common man questions
she could reveal, she could respect.
The tickets for the high balcony —
they were worth a bob or two.
Boys blessed their girlfriends, spoke in Greek,
watching a great picture show,
where cowboys led their lonely lives

uncrowned by Homeric queens, kings,
that lived too long before it all began.
It was time to abandon hope,
time to tear down the high balcony.

The Chicago Aquarium

The weather could be warmer
but children dance in the water
leaving miraculous imprints
on the fountain in Millennium Park
that would cut the legs beneath you —
not that we have faith
in what might redeem ourselves,
redeem the fountain, the aquarium.

It is time to crash the pink reef,
to free the coral river of fish
which have been waiting for our snouts,
our fins, our dexterous escape from sharks,
from the damaged eyes of children
out watching the day,
their dungeon guardians kindly
leading them praying through blessed water,
asking for liberation,
for release from the prison
of sin, mortal sin, venial sin,
no sin at all —
the sins of fathers,
the sins of mothers,
the sin that lay its eggs in their beauty,
in their brains,
in their breasts,
leading them into coral's temptation.

It is time to send electronic mail,
time to send it to ourselves at home.
What is it we shall tell?
What is it these whispers sigh?
Every colour under the stark sun
digests the waters of Chicago,
digests the water of the aquarium.

The end of the world already happened.
Well-behaved dolphins ignored gongs —
better things to do than play mating games,
fragile as hawthorn's hungry flower,
risking a famine of fish and starved seal.
They do not notice who it is they offend.
They back away from poisonous frogs
transported from the mountains of planet earth
which did the dirty dark and found them out
as bold transgressors, as lizards in heat.

I can find the dolphin lacking in love,
lacking but lovely as sea dragons,
the pink leaves of thin divinely fleshed blood,
seeking themselves in the fertile junction
where past and present, present and past,
have the fiercest head for heights.

Leave the dolphins to their treacherous laughter.
Let the score best forgotten be forgotten.
Be at peace in the aquarium.
Men I have loved transformed in its waters
mingle with creatures I'd let devour them
were I not a soft and benevolent shark
breeding with pleasures — with volcanic ash —
in the business of forging watery fire
in the loughs of the Chicago aquarium.

The Japanese Brogue

1

I did not fall down tribal stairs
nor swing from lonely chandeliers
the night the world was stir-crazy.
Instead I read my horoscope,
the sky saturnine as myself,
saying you're due decline and fall.
My limbs were sake doused with milk
they poured from the Japanese brogue,
the finest heifer in Kobe —
a stick to beat my hungry hide,
a drink to quench my silver thirst,
white veal to feed the multitude.

2

Three youngsters in my home town dead.
Rainforest bridge, a falling car.
This has been rough, a red July.
They met their end, one girl, two boys,
solitary machine in flight —
Who saw them tumbling off the earth?
The navigating astronauts,
no fixed abode but speeding safe
in mobile homes, a Donegal
volcano, accounting for three
earthquakes, seismic Umracam.
Their feet fit the Japanese brogue.

3

I've cats who fear the claws of crutch
that feed them milk and chicken cold
as blood that wet itself on floors

that drag betters down, dirty, spilt,
sinful, filthy, Dutch destroyers —
useless, fighting, a pointless game
of love and chance fairly weighted
though provoking laughter, mockery,
insult added to injury —
the broken foot, the breaking heart,
such ritualized nonsense, raw
as wounds in the Japanese brogue.

The Lighthouse Café

Around the Lighthouse Café
the sun rotates.
Cold white wine
has a mind of its own,
a science to the art
of looking at the sky
through rose windows
at the blue stratosphere

This island worships
cathedrals of fuchsia,
bogweed and montbretia,
scented helium
rotating the sun
above the Lighthouse Café.

Tournai

Strange, as the earth bursts open in Tournai.
The cathedral feasts on its five yellow eggs.
Pierced to the pit of roots, Jesse trees sprout.
Their leaves liquefy, quenching the hunger
our dismembered lady shares with her guests.
A Welsh rugby forward, cauliflower-eared,
broke the pietà his wife had just carved.
Making strange, we stayed in the marriage bed.

Wyoming

I will go to Wyoming.
I'll buy myself a beer.
I will go to Wyoming.
I'll wear flowers in my hair.
We will sit in a bar,
drink the earth bone dry.
Setting fire to my hands,
fire to my hair,
they pull wings from me,
my red butterflies.
I will go to Wyoming.
I'll buy myself a beer.
They set fire to my hands,
fire to my hair.

The Chicken Bone

The chicken went untouched.
My cats devoured its bones,
hauled it inside, the orphan flesh.
On broken chairs they sleep,
dreaming of another catch,
the morning claws waiting
for the bread of dawn,
the break of neck, the flute —
the blood of chicken bone.
The chicken went untouched.

The Water Sellers

The candlesticks fell, they broke the plate.
I was eating water with a knife and spoon.
The crack and the crockery were a delta.
In that river I was conceived,
my mother was a goblet of Venice —
my father a German tankard, blue, white.
My family survived on these bare boards.
There was dirty water in our basin,
our dishes were dipped into it.
And the dishes came from Seville,
waiting for silver spouts, pouring water,
pouring songs from my rabble-rousing father.
He sings to save himself in the afterlife.
The afterlife is a place remarkably like Seville.
There are water sellers in Saville —
it is a city rich in almonds.
They serve from delicate Venetian goblets.
They drink out of blue, white German tankards.
They wonder where does it come from?
The water, the rain, the rivers of Spain?

Newmarket

for Rosemary and Stewart Mason

We are passing as if touch is a hoof.
Our cigarettes really should know better.
Were one to live with joy, joy of engaging
in acts of saying nothing but saying
everything, thank God we're expert
at playing mother and playing father.
We would know that starting a family
is tantamount to sharing a secret
we cannot divulge, for our history
rests on winning wars through no careless talk.
Time well spent, money well invested,
I would pay one, two thousand guineas
to fight against the odds that hard, rough scrap
though racing be cancelled at Newmarket.

Leopardstown

for Denis and Roisín Holmes

Above the shopping complex near Leopardstown
angels of the lord danced to demand ransom.
It took the form of fruit-and-nut bars,
Irish Rose, condiments to accompany
meat long past its sell-by date in fridges.
A miracle was called for and came.
Sweetness restored itself to bone and marrow.
Diplomats' wives charmed war out of existence.

China tea sets were shattered into ploughshares.
They worked the fields at the gates of paradise.
Looking at her clever handiwork, smiling,
a dark rose fed the ravenous, lost in grief.
Falling from the skies of India and Spain,
she saw angelic hosts of daughters unborn
singing to four sons, I am Adam, I am Eve,
returning from exile to Leopardstown.

The Lady's Bay

I never leapt
from the high diving board
into the razor,

the silver of sea
that washed the feet
of the Lady's Bay.

Rock

Rain fell on the rock.
Rock washed its two feet.
Feet walked through the dark.
Dark frightened the rock.

Rock fell on the rain.
Rain was washing the dark.
Dark beat its head on the rock.
The dark rock, the rain feet.

Rock fell on the rock.
Rock washed its hair.
Dark walked on two feet.
Rain beat its head.
Rock washed its feet.
Feet walked through dark rain.

Amsterdam

1

Someone nearly drowned that night
walking into the water street.
Did they push or were they fallen?

Might bring them to their senses,
Amsterdam's liquorice sweets —
canals come up to your mitre.

Stupid bastard cannot swim
but can sew a mighty yarn.
All stories end in bye.

Hail the hero of Amsterdam,
stranger than Conglash or Sorn.
All stories end in lies.

2

That night nobody drowned.
Streets were solid beneath our feet.
Went our own way — fell out.

Cocks and arse were north and south.
Senses sharp as greyhound's teeth,
Amsterdam was red as beets.

Never go out on a limb
if it hinders or harms —
let love end, set it free.

Risk the wrath of karma —
these harsh words come from me.
Amsterdam was him.

Rotterdam

There's rain to wet a thousand infants' heads.
Each child christened is to be called Titus.

In the tram someone's stripped bollock-naked.
The last left alive remember the war.

A smell of toasted beef served hot and cold.
The rain falls with good reason on Rotterdam.

Not

My father reading French is not to be.
He needs neither map nor dictionary.
He'll find his way from here to Clonmany,
though bypass Mamore Gap — no reason why.

My mother fears places above sea level.
Blood rushed to the spot, the field, the fell.
Time to say prayers for soul not in hell
nor in heaven, poor pussy down the well.

My father reading French eschews Bible
and Beelzebub. The apocalypse
happens when he's not looking. It's swell
my mother feels duty bound to let rip,
mourning as she does not mourn the lost child
on Mamore Gap, reading French, abandoned, wild.

Calcium

1

You should have seen Mainz in my childhood.
We had our fair share of axe-wielding men.
They provided food for rich and for poor.
As for unknowable Johann Gutenberg,
nothing remotely singled out his father
from the throngs of woodsmelling, bloodied,
strong males who devoured the decent veal
and peas that typified my city's cuisine.
Papa Gutenberg enjoyed a diet of roots
and young meat served up by his young wife.

The women concentrated on recipes,
everything measured accurately,
no such thing as a pinch of ginger,
a few shapes of parsley, a handful
of venison minced into a suitable chew
for men and women dreaming of how
they used to chastise food, beating it
into submission by the use of teeth
rotting into some kind of green,
Protestant face, it being a deeply
held belief among the cognoscenti
of the time that Christianity's schism
would take shape, visible shape
as an identifiable colour
and the likely culprit would be green.

Green was the colour Gutenberg herself —
the mother, I mean, his mother — chose
to insert in her cooking so that
she could poison her husband and children
and thereby escape into the refuge
of a convent where men excused themselves.

The green was in the rotting poultry
she chose to serve — to feed her brood —
brood, a favourite word of Gutenberg's mother —
as a special treat for the Feast of
St Mary Magdalene, beloved by that woman
for reasons perhaps too obvious
or too indecipherable to explain.

All but one of her children she killed.
The husband died roaring as well.
She entered a convent in Mainz.
She took the name Sister Mary of Magdala.
She'd realized her ambition: her fame spread.
Many miracles were verified,
the most famous involved the healing
of a young woman who was the devil.
When she and Satan were separated
the young woman coughed up a manuscript
Sister Mary of Magdala declared
was the true handiwork of Satan.
It was burned in that part of Germany.
The good woman, Gutenberg's mother,
became the patron saint of bonfires.
She is still revered in what remains
of the most Holy Roman Empire.
Her spells split her husband's body in two,
three, four, five — so many pieces,
kidneys, legs, lungs, one eye, two
eyes, two ears, a mouth full of green teeth.

The fool Johann alone survived.
A fool because of his silly habit.
Only his mother noticed this silliness.
Hers was a son who didn't take a blind
bit of notice of what Mother cooked, what

Father suffered. Johann was a boy
content to leave his elders and betters
to the pleasure of their own strange devices.
This meant watching them fuck in the night
pretending Mainz was the Garden of Eden.
Mother and Father are our first parents —
Adam, meet Eve — this time with a difference:
they did not go out to breed and multiply,
earning the lovely bread by sweet sweat
of homely brew, toiling and terrible labour,
roaring their young into existence.
They set out instead to kill children.

2

A fierce disease was eating Mainz,
something to do with bread, with wheat.
Some germ soured inside the young crop.
It took shape in their lonely abdomens,
began to sever the lining, the essence
of the stomach, and wombs lost their reason
to live. In so doing, we re-thought
what reason — what the womb meant.
Many believed both womb and reason
were simply an historical exercise
in excavating powers that be and were.

His mother hermited within the convent,
his holy father dead and buried with
the candlewax remains of melted sons
and soft, soft daughters, Johann continued
as a gesture of childish defiance
to suck his thumb and bite fingernails.
When asked why he persisted in doing so,
he would always reply, I am hungry.

Hungry for what? Starved of affection,
a child turns to his own flesh for comfort —
its warm soup, leafy salad, a piece of fish
that's fresh, leaping, salt still in the sea,
smelling of vinegar and brown paper
and the very text of his well-bitten nails —
thus the boy Gutenberg discovered
that paper — printing — printing on paper
stemmed from the lack of calcium
as he chewed on the stubs of his fingers,
celebrating the starvation of
his mother's hated milk. From this
revelation he wrote his Bible,
the Bible that bears his murdered father's name,
a murder divinely ordained, committed
so that the word of God might reach the eyes
and ears of the known universe.

3

Grown into an old man, Johann Gutenberg
liked to amuse his grandchildren by
sucking their thumbs to ease teething pains.
Their fingers in his mouth make them squirm.
Yet he took great delight in reminding them
he had plotted their future with fingers
and thumbs their fingers and thumbs shot from.
Pointing to the good book, he'd sometimes say,
See that Gutenberg Bible? I wrote it
and it was all because I adored God —
my mother, my father, myself I suffered.
They interrupted him, they answered him,
answered in raucous, piss-taking, shit-smart,
ridiculous, but Gospel-sweet harmony,
You suffered from the lack of calcium.

Montreal

A furlong of snow,
the sky had decided
to stay celibate,
wining, dining,
on dancing feet,
taking pleasure in rivers.
Sleeping on feathers,
water had children,
hard and then soft
as snow in Montreal,
white, black and thaw,
hell for leather,
praying to the sky,
the rivers, the sea.

Patience

I hear my father was pulled to pieces by the white stallions he bred from the brood mares he loved more than his wife and daughters in the days before the revolution.

I find it tempting to contemplate a career as a medium, so I could contact my dead father and ask him if this horrendous rumour bears any resemblance to the truth.

Fortunately, I found shelter in England and I could yield to this temptation with no fear of having to face a tribunal made up of our enemies who would guillotine the likes of me.

I adore the Isle of Wight and, even if my Russian is not up to scratch and I find the natives a mystery, I can still point to the fig trees and let them know they are what I miss most about my past.

I knew a woman once, she spoke in paragraphs, and I do believe it was her disease to be so constrained in memory that the best you could hope to do was to forget.

I remember my mother arguing with my father, and their means of saying everything was silence that attended every meal-time dirty as a potato they scraped skins from with their knives.

They shared a knife the way they shared a bed, and this caused the servants to whisper they must be in love if love is not wrapping flesh around flesh, flesh against flesh.

I believe they never touched and I was conceived from the horses, the white horses stabled in the red barnyard where the revolution was in vogue.

After I was born my father tied me to my mother, struck her arse with a whip and bade her gallop into the unknown with me as her protector.

She did a runner by standing still, and he cursed her for her patience because patience was not a virtue in those days when the Civil War divided families.

I find I'm patient now and I can speak volumes earning a living as an example to those who might desire to contemplate life and need a scapegoat, a warning.

They point me out to their children, and they are white horses, they're my father who no more recognizes me than he did the day I gave the order that he die.

Some leave a pill by the bedside — me, I left a pistol.

Criminals

Say we two were buddies — me jawed-lantern,
innocent, you the wise guy, overacting —
you'd get away with murder, grabbing taxis,
drinking gin, whiskey or sake —
two thousand dollars for a ring?
Forge money, hell's loose and burning.

Grab a freight train to Arizona,
steal a plane, pilot it for free,
turn the sky into silver maize —
I swear I won't be pleased
by the speed of your tall stories,
but beware, they've tapped the phones.

Say you were setting me up —
just say it for convenience —
piss on me to save your skin
when the Feds are closing in —
Think, my love, I'm pretty dense?
Not so, honey, I'm the cops.

Jan Vermeer and a Map of Maynooth

for Bríd O'Doherty

1

I walked down the lonely road to a house in Delft.
There I bought myself bread and came back Catholic,
for my eyes baptized themselves in locusts and honey
since my flesh broke its fast to receive Communion.

My knees knelt in penance, sorry for my father
who curses my wedding night, the sheets, my milk,
my bride white — better to lie with the bad whore,
Babylon,
than this Papist bitch in heat, though her tongue be pearls.

We had children, my bride, myself, bodies of paper.
My wife paid our wet nurse with the price of a hat
she had stolen from her fat sister — I fancied that one, so
red —
but I said nothing: this was not the done thing in Delft.

That ludicrous sister passed me the map of a town
in Ireland, called Maynooth, somewhere in County Kildare.
It's whispered the streets there lead to God's temple
where you can find lost love — my father's lost love.

This confirmed my suspicions — don't leave Delft —
don't take Holy Orders — don't drink in dirty cafés —
do not touch wine that costs an arm and a leg —
do not have dreams of Asia, of marrying China.

I married in Delft and we had blue children.
They cupped their faces and spouted scalding water.
Yes, they were dead but they'd served their purpose.
I learned to read fortunes in the leaves of their cheeks.

2

As I watched them die, my extreme children,
I washed them in the oil of St Anne,
the Virgin's mother giving birth to time and death,
whispering you will let time defy your death,
Jan Vermeer, stretched out for life on the map of Maynooth:
stick it in a painting, the clergy will love you.
Make this street divine: above all avoid accidents,
loveliness of God you won't locate in a map.
Their hero is silken, a Thomas, a patriot of doubt —
they gather in his castle to drink demonic milk.
Avoid the milk of devils, avoid the wall of China
though it is visible from the moon as are motorways
of Belgium. I have never been to China. Belgium
does not exist — do I exist? What are motorways?
Are they visible from the sun, the roads we travel?
Time and death looked at me, laughing in my face.
They saw there the map of my dying father.
They saw there the map of my dying mother.
They saw the map of Delft, the map of Maynooth.
My eyes saw the map of the moon and the sun.
In the sun my father can be seen from the moon —
in the moon my mother is the wall of China.
My father's tears drench the motorways of Belgium.
My mother's a shadow dancing in the sun —
revealing Jan Vermeer who died far too young
leaving behind a house full of wife and kids
who'll never see the sacred town of Maynooth
where God was born if you were to believe
that chancer, the same Vermeer, who glimpsed paradise
in the Holy Orders of the still town of Delft.
Having seen the truth, I turned my back and fled.
My arse was white though no sun shone from it.

3

I let my wife caress that arse like a lost lover.
My body, it danced on dangerous motorways.
That is my way of meeting my father on the moon.
He'd touched my mother, caressed her with men's hands.

Centuries ago these hands traced the map of Maynooth.
Frightened of touch, frightened of the moon,
frightened of night on motorways in Belgium,
frightened above all of the map of my mother.

I will smash a lamp and decorate my hair
with the linked petals of the bulb and the sun.
I will tell my father tales he never told me.
Dress him in fur nightlight licks yellow.

Thus in dreams came the voice of Jan Vermeer,
his vision the moonscaped motorways of Belgium,
knowing such a place does not yet exist,
no more than Maynooth where Vermeer lies hiding.

Sans Souci Park

in memory of Twinkle Egan

It costs a fortune to live there now.
Absolute fortune and ravishing darkness.
A place to hunt more than hart and hind
before they die — before we die — good news,
bad news, the gospel truth to give and take,
the red of brick, the sigh of why it all starts
in the echo that fills Sans Souci Park,
in the echo that fills Sans Souci Park.

There was a time, I remember it well,
my boot took its peasant vengeance and bins
of Booterstown went flying — flesh and fowl,
skin and tin, glass and scissors, paper, rock —
I took my chance and defiled Sans Souci,
I kicked its lids like silver footballs, far
from the echo that fills Sans Souci Park,
from the echo that fills Sans Souci Park.

I was Hannibal setting out to raze.
All I had to do was cross the crazed Alps,
shoot the elephants, kiss my gun,
create consternation in Sans Souci.
Blossoms in snow, my soldiers melted —
I grew respectable — a cultured asset,
echoing gardens scenting Sans Souci Park,
echoing gardens scenting Sans Souci Park.

There is milk for many in Sans Souci.
A herd of sorrow devours the sweet grass.
The Hindu gods have made habitation
in the Ganges of lawns, the influx of birds —
the wings, the bones of hard daisy chains
bearing witness to whatever happens within

the echo filling all of Sans Souci Park,
the echo filling all of Sans Souci Park.

I search for hart, for hind, for nightingale,
through ravishing darkness of Sans Souci,
endangered protector, species of sound,
in the echo that is Sans Souci —
the Ganges is flooding through the gutters,
I shelter myself, man and boy, pup and cur
in the echo that is Sans Souci Park,
in the echo that is Sans Souci Park.

You should see the price now in Sans Souci.
The rich find shelter, they're welcome to it.
They can sing like larks, like strange nightingales
lamenting lost cities like Tyre and Sidon
playing elephants whose ivory keys
smell of lost roses and a Ganges of grief
drowning the gardens of Sans Souci Park,
drowning the gardens of Sans Souci Park.

Dulse

A mermaid clutched my father and breathed in his ear,
This is the way we choose to leave the earth.

A sinner, a sailor, a man of every port,
I do believe he tried his best to make the marriage last.

Sent from Atlantis to forage soft dulse,
she was my mother, my father was dulse.